WomensWords

Through The Eyes Of A Woman

Edited by

Heather Killingray

First published in Great Britain in 1998 by
WOMENSWORDS
1-2 Wainman Road, Woodston,
Peterborough, PE2 7BU
Telephone (01733) 230746
Fax (01733) 230751

HB ISBN 1 86188 626 8
SB ISBN 1 86188 621 7

FOREWORD

Although we are a nation of poetry writers we are accused of not reading poetry and not buying poetry books: after many years of listening to the incessant gripes of poetry publishers, I can only assume that the books they publish, in general, are books that most people do not want to read.

Poetry should not be obscure, introverted, and as cryptic as a crossword puzzle: it is the poet's duty to reach out and embrace the world.

The world owes the poet nothing and we should not be expected to dig and delve into a rambling discourse searching for some inner meaning.

The reason we write poetry (and almost all of us do) is because we want to communicate: an ideal; an idea; or a specific feeling. Poetry is as essential in communication, as a letter; a radio; a telephone, and the main criteria for selecting the poems in this anthology is very simple: they communicate.

This book contains an excellent collection of poems written by only women. We are giving women the chance to give us all an insight into their busy interesting lives.

Women have fought through most oppression but in a few areas of life some still exist. This is the topic of many of these poems, questions, equality and their restricted opportunities. Many also are on a positive theme such as the wonderful experience of being a mum or the special relationships they share with people because they are a woman.

This book can be enjoyed by both men and women and may help us all to have a better insight into issues that are valuable to women.

CONTENTS

The Birth

How beautiful my love is!
A rose all newly opened in the storm,
Magnificent as black clouds about a half-frozen moon,
Soft as dampened lambs new-born,
As music through the trees has passed
When slow the weary sun burns red
Drift to the lily pond, soft shadows cast,
And song-filled frogs sit unafraid,
Where floats the half-drowned dragonfly
Gauzy wings hung limp and sad
Quivering and turning golden with the sun
Till he lies one flame all glorified
And flame and light and death are one.
Tufty clouds like downy puff-balls loose
Dance across the star-specked blue
Flirt and tease the ripples as they choose:
Rest and drift and part and woo
Then suddenly decide to float away
And leave the stars to call the death of day.

S K Baker

Remember When?

Do you remember when we were kids the games we used to play?
Spits and strides and skipping to rhymes that we would say.
House to let, enquire within and *Girl Guides dressed in blue,*
I liked it best when someone's mother wound the rope - did you?
Whip and top and *hopscotch* and sometimes *tin can squat,*
The lads played that one usually, we didn't - not a lot.
'What time is it Mr Wolf?' we'd chant and scream as we ran away,
That's a game you never see the children play today.
Cowboys and Indians, *statues, cops and robbers too,*
I don't remember being bored, there seemed so much to do.
Do you remember watching for the lamplighter to come?
He came each night as it grew dark to turn the street lights on.
He carried a long pole with him and lit each lamp in turn,
The pole was used to light the gas that made the mantle burn.
In winter when the snow came we'd sledge or make a slide,
Then skid along the track we made - 'It's just like glass' we cried.
We'd go home later, wet and cold, to sit by a roaring fire,
With tingling toes and fingers we'd watch the flames grow higher.
Our socks and gloves were all spread out around the hearth to dry,
Our toes and fingers hurt so much that sometimes we would cry.
But still the next day, after school, we'd play outside once more,
And end up wet and freezing cold just like we had before.
And O! The Plots and Christmases, Easters and Whitsun too,
All had a special magic that made some dreams come true.
I could go on forever on things we did back then,
And every phrase would start with - do you remember when?

B Austick

My Pregnancy

I got my result in July '94
I was so shocked I nearly fell through the floor
It wasn't long before I started to look round
Weight was piling on by the pound
I had a routine scan and told everything was fine
I couldn't believe the baby on the screen was mine
I got bigger and bigger I thought I would burst
I couldn't get in decent clothes, that's when
I cursed

My waters broke a month before I was due
I was stunned as I'd just gone to the loo
I booked into hospital and was taken to the ward
I soon made friends so I didn't get bored

It was the night after I eventually became a mum
I went deaf but I definitely wasn't dumb
We had decided we'd call him Kyle
I'd had an easy labour but had a painful pile
Through lack of sleep I was so tired
Wherever we went Kyle was admired

Now he is older and walking about
He's now talking but prefers to shout
I love Kyle more than words can say
He gets more mischievous and cheekier every day
I wouldn't change a thing he is a typical boy
As he is loveable with it, he is a child to enjoy

Deborah Thomas

The River Thames

The River Thames is very special
It has a lifestyle of its own
There are many little boats
Cruising up and down her every day
With people sitting and standing on their decks
Looking at the wondrous sights
Along the river banks

They see the great Thames Barrier
Stretching out in all its height
And in all its grace
They see the Tower of London
And learn about the Traitors' Gate
There's the big majestic Tower Bridge
Which opens up its gate
For the big ships to pass through

There is the naval ship the Belfast
That people go on every day to view
Other bridges, also span the Thames
All as old as time itself
We have Greenwich Park and Richmond
Kew Gardens, Hampton Court, so full of history

There are all the floating restaurants
That you can have a meal and drink on
Whilst relaxing for a while
People live on boats along its banks
Wanting freedom for a life
Old Father Thames goes on and on
It looks so peaceful and serene
Wildlife swim upon it

Plants and flowers grow close by
Trees their branches they hang down
God we thank you very much
For the lovely River Thames

Jodie Moore

UNTITLED

I shall visit the same old familiar places
and see many of the same old faces.
But though I sit and long and stare
your face my dear, will not be there.
But I shall seem not to care, I shall be gay
I will laugh with the others and say,
'Remember him, oh too grand now he is
to drink with us and laugh like this?'

Now you've made your way from our gay crowd
but once you were just as noisy and loud.
That was the time when most I loved you
and foolishly thought I would always be with you.
But you had other ideas, other plans, other aims
you grew up and advised us to do the same.
Time you said we went our way to far off lands
and so we drifted apart like many grains of sand.

The tears were hard, many that I wept
but still a place in my heart I have kept.
Should you return and need me again now
to wipe the journey's dust from your tired brow.

I shall be here in the same old place
waiting for your return - just in case
You are missing the love of the old crowd
whose noise and laughter is just as loud.

Mary C Guilfoyle

TWO YEARS OLD

Tiny little pattering feet, always running, running;
Piping infant voices calling 'Coming, coming!'
Eyes wide open, filled with love and trust;
Wilful stubborn minds, insisting 'I must, I must!'

Busy hands and fingers, exploring far and near,
Open arms embracing, knowing they are dear.
Endless patience needed, day after day;
Lovingly moulding precious lumps of clay.

Lovingly moulding innocent pliable minds;
Endeavouring to make them a gift to humankind.
Growing little bodies, becoming strong and free;
Endless hours of wonder in everything they see.

Days of fun and laughter, night-times of tears;
Gentle voices murmuring, banishing their fears.
Two years old, and learning, learning how to live;
Loving, laughing, crying, yet always they give.

Give us happiness and love, sorrow and pain;
And yet, through it all, ours is the gain.
Ours the gift of cherishing this little one so dear;
Ours the gift of sharing, throughout the coming years.

Catherine Riley

TRAPPED

A lonely young girl
inwardly trying to reach out
but she found it impossible to ask for help

She wrestled daily with the image in the mirror
and pleaded for help
but no-one could hear her

Locked in a world where she could not eat
she barely walked
she could only creep

Distorted images before her eyes
testing her sanity
making her cry

Everything edible had to go
It brought too much pain
and she should know

Pulled in one way
and then in another
she covered her ears to escape the thunder

This lonely girl
in her prison cell
devoid of feelings
she's just a shell

Samantha Stephens

GENTLE

e is fairy gold,
slips, and fades away when held too tightly by any jealous bands,
ll die if told that it must always stay,
lows most brightly in gentle open hands.

lovely thing turns into lifeless dust when deprived of care.
ower will lose its scent when pressed,
d the wing of a butterfly crushed,
never flies the air again,
its life is spent.

I will hold this heart with a silken bind,
stronger than a band of steel could ever be,
fearing it may part will keep me in his mind,
more fast than a hand of iron,
but, gently.

Sal Magundi

SIRENS

It's part of the loving you said
This hiding in dark damp places
Where rats snicker before they bite
Fighting in alleyways
Running from strangers
Who hide in your shadow waiting patiently to rape your sanity

But it was me
I suffered the table and the knife
The blinding lights that burn to the very core
The memory of the wires snapping at my skin

But that's the price of the loving you said
So we run, never daring to dream of coming home

I'm scared, I'm alone, and I'm frightened
I run with my love for you hanging around
Me like a banner of protection
Hoping the evilness of this life will not seep through it

And as the sirens sound
Cold and breathless in the dirt
I lay at your feet exhausted
And I wonder if my body and my will
Can last as long as this love for you.

Nicola Y Murphy

De Ya Ken

Ha ya got a penny for the gas
Or can ya lend a cup a sugar for our Sal
Me ma's away at market, me little brither's starving
Me da's at the boozer and the dogs are all barking

But they were happy days, de ya ken?

I dinne what to make for ya piece
Nither a lot of grub in the hoose
Aw, let's not worry hen, I found a halfpenny
And we buy some speck fruit and a wee dram

Oh we were happy then, de ya ken?

The weans are all a wailing
Your granda on his ship a sailin',
Will he ne'er come back and take up the sack
Down the docks to get some coal
We'll not tell a living soul.

But we were happy then, de ya ken?

Away to church and then confession
Fr Gilligan at his session
Has to gag hisself from laughing
At the tales that come a passin'
Three Hail Mary's and one Our Father
My, we did get in a lather

Aye those were happy days de ya ken?

S Burke

STAND UP TALL

Oh, stand up tall - turn, face the light
And let them see you in your plight.
Is accusation bringing shame
And, if it is, then who's to blame?
It's you because you will not fight.

Why can't you see you're in the right?
You've done no wrong, in God's dear sight
And yet you cringe in shameful pain -
Oh, stand up tall!

Hold on to friendship very tight -
It is a gift with strength and might;
It will not sully any name -
Nor even yet will bear a stain -
But rather it will bring delight.
Oh, stand up tall!

Alison M Rowan

Grandma's Eyes

So what will you tell . . .
your children's children
when they speak
of lovers
an addiction
the power of music
hypnotics of drink.
The first time they open their eyes
to find the open skies
the only bedroom ceiling
they can see.

Will you tell the truth
pain and pleasure
youth
Will you have to lie . . .
I think I will smile
and leave them to find
what they can . . .
in my eyes.

Hannah Campagna

The Housewife

Her last child is safe at school
Her son cycles for a lecture in Cambridge
Her husband of twenty odd years begins another surgery -
It's Monday 9am so it must be housework.

She lingers over a second coffee
Trying to galvanise herself upstairs.
She begins with the bathroom -
Ennui takes over.
She was doing this at 9.30am for years
And are there years ahead?
Who knows . . .
She dusts and vacuums and tidies
And a stifling loneliness envelopes her.
She becomes desperate to finish her tasks
And get out -
Into the air, see people, life, the real world, movement.
Away from the sterile, claustrophobic, the stunting,
Repetitive, boring, thankless chores.
But it is her 'job'
She has to work to fill her days
To justify her existence.
She has a deep need to care, to be needed,
To be wanted.
Or has she?
Who wants a worn out shell
Desperate to tell someone she cleaned the windows today?
Pathetic . . .
Still it's nice to come home
To a clean house, with flowers,
And a casserole in the oven!

Ann Upton

A WOMAN'S PLACE

A woman's work is never done, is a phrase that's often said,
And from rising in the morning, till you go back to bed,
There is washing waiting to be done, and then the ironing too,
Cleaning, scrubbing, mending, cooking, and that's to name a few!
We raise the kids, look after husbands, garden, decorate and such,
The days are never long enough to accomplish quite so much!
We bake, make jams and chutney, we are really versatile,
Then say I'm just a housewife - it has to make you smile!

Women are the backbone of the country, it really would collapse,
Without the volunteers and carers, grinding to a halt, and then perhaps
Men would get to grips with all the problems. If we withdrew our labours,
And not say we wouldn't understand, and think they do us favours!
For it's the women of the countries who have to clear up all the mess,
While men go on fighting, causing bother, just to prove their macho-ness!
There are women in high places now - doctors, managers we trust,
We can almost manage without men - but can they manage without *us?*

Kathleen Adams

I AM PREDATOR

I stand alone in that quiet place
I hear you before I see you
Your eerie shriek pierces the quietness
Song birds stay silent in the hot afternoon
Hidden from you under leaves of green
Aware of the predator on the wing
Sheep start and run from your cry
Your silent wings catch the warm air
You can see all things from your flight in the sky
Can you see me in my turmoil?
I can see you
I can see me
Why can I not fly away on warm air filled wings?
Away from the turmoil within
You soar above the trees crying
I am here on earth crying
Your cry is of domination
My cry is of despair
You are invincible on the air, no-one can touch you
You can escape
I am here trapped within this body and mind I hate
The only way out is a dishonourable death
Yet you don't think this way
Your way is to survive at all costs
Has my life come to mean so little, that the only alternative is death
I am not aware of any predator except man
I am my only predator.

Hilary Jean Clark

THE SEVENTH COMMANDMENT

Why send him my way if he's so out of reach,
Is this a temptation intending to teach?
Will pain make me stronger, will tears cleanse my soul
How many denials before I am whole?

I'd buried my dreams and I'd improvised fate,
Why send him now when you know it's too late?
And what if I choose just this once to rebel
Would you sanction my end as forever in hell?

If indulging this love that I'd dreamt of for years,
Would you harden my heart to other soul's tears?
But if I decided this price was too high
Would you hold me in love when it's my turn to cry?

So if love's not allowed, will you then take my place
Will you wrap your arms around him and make sure he's safe?
Then close his heart to me, beg my heart be still,
For that's what I need to submit to your will.

Patricia Frost

My Other Garden

Who has not dreamt of gardens strangely still
Where mystery mingles with the scented air,
Where winding paths lead to some hidden spring,
Or to an arbour overgrown with briars?
But dreams disperse when daylight breaks the spell
And then no magic lurks in my small plot.
Here rule two potentates of tender age
Who tilt and joust upon the battered lawn.
No mystery here, but unexpected things:
A plastic sword thrust through the laurel bush,
A mini spaceship in the lupin bed.
But when night treads the garden path once more
And conjures unknown shapes from bush and tree,
And leaves become dark lace against the sky,
My garden small lies rocked in mystery.

Margaret Gregory

UNTITLED

You worked hard to bring us up
We were so very poor
You loved us all and cared for us
Who could ask for more.

When Dad died you went away
It nearly broke my heart
Every day for over a year
Uncontrollable tears would start.

When you were taken to hospital
How could we leave you there
You didn't want to stay
What a burden we have to bear.

How could we ignore your cries and pleas
Not to leave you in that place
Poor little 'Mumsy darling'
I'll never forget your face.

Alone and with a broken heart
It took over three years to die
No-one there to comfort you
Again I start to cry.

My dearest darling Mum
It is very true
No other father or mother
Could do any more than you.

How can we make it up to you
Dear sweet gentle Mother
I know that you would like
For us to love each other.

M K Wheeler

MY FOREVER FRIEND

You came to be mine when I was a tot,
And I loved you dear Snowy, oh such a lot,
Together with Dad we'd roam through the lanes,
And enter gymkhanas with all kinds of games.
Sometimes you'd give rides to my friends in the cart,
It wasn't too long till you'd stolen their hearts.
You were not a thoroughbred but my you were fine,
I saw all your beauty because you were mine.
Such big gentle eyes, a strong handsome head,
You'd visit our garden and attack Mum's rose-bed.
You hated the stable and loved to be free,
But when Mum's car pulled up you'd come running to me.
Your strong sturdy legs, your long flowing mane,
To lose you my boy brought such sorrow and pain.
My pal how I loved you, so precious, so bold,
I just didn't think you would ever grow old.
You retired from shows to a life full of leisure,
A 'thank you' from me, for you brought me such pleasure.
Now God has a pasture up high in the sky,
With the greenest of grass for when great horses die.
I think of you there as each new day appears,
Sometimes the memories re-start all my tears.
I fancy I hear you as I stand at the gate,
I call out your name, and then I just wait.
I fancy I hear you whinny and neigh,
As you thunder on up for some food and some hay.
Your body now rests in the field you loved most,
Soon an oak tree will grow with the strength of your ghost.
Always dear Snowy you'll live on in my heart,
Forever I'll love you, as I vowed from the start.

Audrey Tully

School Days

I really hate these mornings.
'But why?' I hear you say.
Because the weekend's over
And I'm back at school today.
There I was in a wonderful sleep
All snug and warm in bed
When my dreams were finally shattered
By the alarm clock near my head!
A leisurely breakfast, not a chance,
There really isn't time
'Cos you know you're in big trouble
If you're not at school by nine.
Endless maths, English and French,
Geography, history too . . .
I hope these teachers understand
What our brains are going through!
But now Monday's almost over
Four more days and Friday's here,
I always feel much better
When I know the weekend's near.
They say that school's important
If you want to get ahead,
But ask me where I'd rather be . . .
It's back at home in bed!

Susan Shaw

Diana - A Princess Of The People

We couldn't know her deeply she was only ours to share
We only saw the press portrayal of 'How and When and Where'
She met with people old and young, the rich, the poor, the lame
And deep into the heart it was to people that she came

It happened, oh so suddenly the shock so hard to bear
The loss, one deeply felt that had a nation in despair
By press and media hounded no life to call her own
The money changing hands made her suffer by renown

Her every move reported was like a TV soap
It was to be her ending that no-one could have thought
Sunflowers, roses, lilies all were brought to share
Just how a nation loved her just how a nation cared

The Queen paid tribute on TV of warmth and inspiration
Her devotion to the boys and sorrow with the nation
Earl Spencer spoke with anger of press and ruined lives
But media and drunk driving brought the end of Diana's life

The night before the funeral was shared by young and old
They lit their candles of the night and watched the dawn unfold
Then came that final day for all, the time to say farewell
To a special person in our lives we all had shared as well

The throwing of the flowers the jangling horses' hooves
The public tears a flowing as doves flew off the roofs
The lilies on the standard slight wavering in the wind
The posy to a mummy touched hearts across the land

Her coffin's final journey to Althorp place of peace
A silence spread around the world her love will never cease
Your resting place is fitting, an island in a lake
In peace and new tranquillity for your spirit's flight to take.

Carol Younger

Let Us Feel Safe

Every day in the paper,
You read of murder and rape,
What is wrong with these people?
Why are they so full of hate?

Women fear of being out,
On the streets late at night,
Keeping to pathways,
That are well alight.

Not knowing who could be lurking,
Around the next corner,
When someone appears,
Without any warning.

It's probably someone innocent,
Who's out for fresh air,
But it still makes you wary,
When you see them stood there.

Is this how we've to live?
Always in fear,
Will the streets ever be safe?
Will these evil people always be here?

The women who are victims,
Are as innocent as you and me,
Their lives ruined forever,
They will never be free.

Michelle Wilson

Peace

To walk in peace throughout your life
Takes wisdom, thought and care
Letting go of all the hurts
Then letting love reign there

Peace is something we can find
When love of self steps in
No more abuse from other's use
A sense of self within

There comes a time when we must know
Enough's been said that's wrong
The only person we can change
Is self and what we've done

To find your peace, know yourself
Like what you find inside
The right to choose and say 'No'
Let peace and love abide

Brenda Whitby

Is It Me

I look into the mirror, whose face do I see
I'm looking really hard, surely that's not me.
My hair is going grey, there's wrinkles in my skin
My face it looks much plumper, when once it was quite thin.
Where have all the years gone, the time has gone so quick
The days of my youth gone past, my how the time does tick.
I take another look, in the mirror just to see
That the stranger staring back, is really really me.
The grey hair and the wrinkles and every little line
And so I must accept, that yes this face is mine.

Teresa Garnham

Grandma - 1857-1930

Her starched white apron reached the ground,
And as she walked it made the sound
Of crackle and pop, rustle and creak,
And where her belt rubbed, an occasional squeak!

Where was she going, this grandma of mine?
To see a sick neighbour and take her some wine
Made from the flowers that grew in the field,
Which this year were prized for their very good yield.

Her covered tray was laden with food,
To cheer her friend and do her good,
What she carried was savoury and sweet,
Calves food jelly, and home cured meat.

For a pig hung down from her kitchen beam,
Recently killed and washed in the stream,
An apple jelly, new seed cake,
Gathered together for friendship's sake.

Her tray was heavy, but did she moan?
No, she smiled as she set off from home -
Patted her hat, and straightened her skirt
And popped a clean hanky inside her shirt.

Victoria reigned for most of her life,
But, being a kindly farmer's wife
She shared her lot with those less blessed -
The poor, sick, lonely and distressed.

Kathleen C White

A LETTER TO SANTA

Mum says it's nearly Christmas, such happy days ahead,
'It's time to write your letters boys, we'll write them before bed.'
I sit and stare, with pen in hand, I can't seem to get started,
The one thing really on my mind, is Dad and Mum are parted.

I duly start to write my list, I know that's what I should,
A bike, a car and train-set, please Santa if I'm good.
And if it's not too much to ask, for Xmas what I'd like,
Is all of us together, I don't mind about the bike.

For Mum and Dad to laugh again, and Daddy to come back,
To stay for good and be with us, I'd love that in your sack.
My Mummy says you're magic, and I believe you must be,
If you can't manage toys as well, please, just bring back my Daddy.

Sonia Mills

DEATH IS

Death is
Death is unjust
Death is unanswerable
Death does not even bother to smile in triumph.

But oh the need to spring upon it
And catch it by the throat
And beat and beat its cruel shrouded head into the ground
Until -
There's no until.

For all the beating in the world will not afford
The slightest touch of vanished hand
Or voice.

Death is

Ira in mortem conturbat me.

Christine Kennett

LOVE

Love was beautiful, at 21 years of age
Two bodies joined as one.
Love was so special that very first time,
A new experience, blowing your mind,
Neither of you knowing what to expect
Both of you anxious, and yet,
You remember every single word that he said,
Long, long after you got out of bed,
Not just for a day, a week, a year,
Something special you hold very dear.
Both of you knowing you're committed to each other,
Never thinking of taking another.
Throughout your life this is what binds you together,
You weather the storms, the good, the bad,
Whatsoever.
Life throws some really awful things at you,
Some so bad you just don't know what to do.
But, over thirty years down the line,
Love is still special after all this time.
Love is still special, love is still fun,
Love is still beautiful, at almost fifty one.

Pat Dring

THE FIRST FATHER'S DAY WITHOUT YOU

It hasn't been so very long
since we were last together
the final week I spent with you
I'll cherish and will treasure
I'm very glad we had that time
to tie up all loose ends
to focus on important things
that 'live on' when 'life' ends
We always had a special bond
although we had our clashes
but even in our stormy times
we knew each other mattered.
I'm really going to miss you Dad
your warmth and sense of fun
I always knew you loved me
when all was said and done
there's no one in this world like you
you certainly were unique
but now you're free of stress and pain
you moved on as if from sleep
and every time I think of you
your funny ways and what you'd do
It really fills my heart with pride
In those reflecting times I set aside
It hurts when some things start to dim
then out of nowhere it's clear again
No time or circumstance could erase
the difference to my life you made
for death and time can't break this tie
built up in a lifetime with you and I
Thanks for how you loved me *Dad*
you were the very best I could have had.

Alison Kathryn Lewis

Decision

Someone you love a lot is dying
From a serious disease which is quickly spreading
Do you tell them you know they'll get better?
If you do, you know you are lying
Could you warn them of their fate
As death approaches it might be too late
The decision to tell them is too hard to make
This tragic news we cannot break
Instead we pretend they are going to get better
Just tell them we love them by writing a letter.

Elaine May

SOUNDS OF CHILDHOOD

Can you remember, when you were a child
The sounds of summer noises?
The buzzing of bees, the bleat of lambs
And laughing human voices.

Brisk breeze in the grass near the river bank,
The gentle low of a cow.
A skylark's song as it soared on high,
Can you remember them now?

Slap-flapping sail of a boat on the pond,
The squeaking chains on the swings.
The roar of a harvester in the field,
Can you remember these things?

The pitter patter of light falling rain,
The silence as day grows dark.
Soft hooting of owls in the woodland trees,
Cooing of doves from the park.

A kitten's purr as you stroke its sleek coat,
Your spinning top whizzing round.
The *whack* of a ball as it meets the bat,
Can you remember that sound?

When you grow old, you remember again,
As you watch new babies learn.
Soon they will grow up, grow old and forget
And then it will be their turn,

To listen once more and say to themselves,
When they hear their young ones call
In reply to sounds they only can hear,
'Ah, yes! I remember it all.'

Mary Dinnis

I Caught That Glance

Your face glistening with the heat
of the kitchen.
Churning out china and steam.
Endless plates of comfort and coffee,
achieving that Italian dream.
Smoking half a cigarette during half
a conversation.

Pulling intensely on the smoke
and half-heartedly on my words.
I caught that glance you gave her,
serving coffee and that look.

In the dim light you spin around the tables
emptying ashtrays full of other people's fears.
Grasp my reality, not a stranger's.
Your sweat and my tears.
'We need time to ourselves,' you say,
as you're glancing her way.

Pulling intensely on the smoke
and half-heartedly on my words.
Your eyes traced down her neck to ankle
while waiting for her to pay.

Anne Phillips

The Glory Of Hope

The Glory of Hope comes after oppression
Doors open afresh, a new life, a new lesson
To learn *how* to live - charge taken again.
Duties upheld - to demur and refrain
From battle and quarrel - good government's in session.

There are problems ahead, experience was lost
How decisions are made, and the ultimate costs
Of changing the ways for all to attain
The Glory of Hope

Love one's neighbours, learn tolerance to trade
With those who oppressed - be willing *not* made
To do what is right for mankind as a whole
There's need for a model, an exact correct role.
All that is done in the future must aid
The Glory of Hope.

M C Cobb

Dear Tom . . .

When she cut off the strings
She said you were trained,
In what? That's what I want to know.
You leave out the bread,
The cheese and the milk,
And there's holes in your socks - which I sew.
The clothes which are dumped
At the side of our bed -
Who do you think picks them up?
The Hoover? The dog? The washing fairy?
I'm telling you I've had enough.
I'm sick and tired of running your baths,
And ignoring all your bad habits.
Your burps and farts could energise a village
And what happened to shagging like rabbits?
I thought when the kids finally left home
We could travel, just you and me.
But all you do is sit in that chair
Shouting: 'Mary, what's for tea?'
I'm 48 and I want my own life
And that's the reason I'm leaving you.
I'm joining a cult in Milton Keynes,
They're friendly and cook all their own food.
I've left a list with Mrs Hill
Explaining how to switch things on.
Good luck and do not think of me
For I won't be missing you Tom.

Lindsay Jennings

TRAPPED

Look in the eyes of your grandmother, then look in the
eyes of a child.
She will be like your grandmother in just a little while,

A child is running in a field, the wind blowing, tussling,
her hair, rosy cheeks soft as silk you see no wrinkles
there.

A young girl going dancing, twirling around the floor,
look in the eyes of your grandmother, she can't do that
anymore.

Here comes the bride so happy, so very much in love,
In a church she makes her marriage vows to her man and
God above.

A mother cradling her baby.
The wheels of time go round, everything is oh so quiet,
you cannot hear a sound.

Looking in the mirror, give a little sigh, look in the
eyes of your grandmother.
She isn't there, it is I.

Yvonne Magill

Just Jump

I can see you, captured one,
Dancing upon the spot,
Running around in circles,
Frustrated at your lot.

You're not the first or the last,
I've seen it all before;
Men and women, boys and girls,
Sin-battered and so sore.

O'er Jerusalem I've wept
And longed with all my heart
To hold her in loving arms
That of me she might be part.

Jerusalem would not come,
It's just the same with you.
Unless you will come to me
There's no more I can do.

Jump off your self-made cliff-top,
I wait with open arms.
You may feel it's suicide,
Afraid you'll come to harm.

You'll never know, till you jump,
What love I have in store.
Try it once and you will soon
Suffer alone no more.

Winifred Rickard

TRUE LOVE

His blue eyes look into mine,
The long eyelashes flicker.
The telepathy begins,
I know what he requires of me,
To sing a song.

An old song I begin,
We sit hand in hand.
His exquisite fingers
A miracle of creation.
I finish my refrain
And know I have found true love.

Can anyone explain why
Grandmothers are so boring?

M J Grout

The Timepiece

Time to rise from our bed the alarm has just said
Now our time we utilise according to family size
For us time is of the essence
All members requiring our presence

The timepiece in the hall
Is impressive it stands so tall
Its face is not given to indecision
With hands that move to precision
The pendulum swings below saying tick tock tick tock
This timepiece is known as a clock
Though the rhythm is a comforting sound
To this clock our lives are bound

Time never sleeps, it just passes by
There's a time to be born and a time to die
A time to laugh and a time to cry
Time flies, it really does, except when waiting for a bus
Time we cannot spurn whichever way we turn
We've more time now the kids have gone
But the clock in the hall still ticks on

Yet time can be our saviour
If we choose not to deploy our labour
We just say 'Sorry we have not time'
This being the accepted line
If at a party we are not amused
We use 'time' again to be excused
Time will always dictate to us
No time now to make a fuss
But it would be nice to have a slot
And stay in a place that time forgot.

June Egan

THE TIGRESS

A tigress in a business suit
With killer instinct bared
Claws to gouge out any deal
No victim ever spared
Hunting for the thrill of it
That lingered smell of fear
A tingle of excitement
As the victory draws near
Once purring like a pussy cat
Now power brings its roar
She pads around the boardroom
An executive and more
A woman with a nose for business
Fire in her eyes
Carnivorous and hungry
One whom no man terrifies.

Kim Montia

JANIE-LEE

You gave me sleepless nights at first,
I was too proud to care.
You cried out in your hunger
And I was always there.
I fed you rich milk from my breast,
And wiped your sticky face,
And knew at last, in the lonely world,
I'd finally found my place.

The child that swelled in my belly once
Is nigh on seven years.
She's shown me joy and caused me pain,
And I've cried many tears.
I never knew I'd give so much
Of my own life away,
But I find I'll give it willingly,
Just to make her smile and say
Endearing childish nothings
That make me want to weep,
And the promises she makes to me
That my heart she will keep.

I love to see her growing up,
Although it means away,
But much as I'll depend on her
I'll never make her stay.
In years to come I'll have to share
With others, boy and man
But since I am her constant now
I'll enjoy her while I can.

Karen Brown

HARBOUR LIGHTS

Darkness descends as the ship takes its place,
turning in darkness the sea now to face.
Harbour lights flicker to create a magical sight,
as the ship gathers speed sailing into the night.
Standing to watch as the wind takes your breath,
leaving the safe harbour for the dark sea's depth.
Hands growing colder gripping the rail as the
wind pinches faces making them pale.
People begin to leave the darkened cold deck,
as harbour lights fade then disappear like a speck.
Bravely the vessel charges far out to sea, into a
cloak of darkness swept now are we.
Away from safety sailing into the deep, to sense
mother nature moving, too restless for sleep.
Out in the wilderness miles out to sea, everyone
knows that in charge God has to be.
Pulses racing, hearts skip a beat, as tossed by the
sea, decks move under our feet
Just when we fear never again will we see land,
comes the reassurance of God's guiding hand.
Engines are cut, we begin to slow down, there
in the distance glow lights like a crown.
Harbour lights beckon now from a different
shore, as we arrive safely, back home once more.

Veronica Black

BLUNT RAZOR

I look down on my legs,
Yesterday's stubble;
And I cannot show myself to you,
Like I have something to hide,
And when I look at my face
Shadows haunt my lips and my eyes
My hair freaks around my head,
Freaks around truths I am hiding from myself
I try and hide it all
For you.

My blunt razor, which has no place in my room
Make-up, that I never wear
The hairs on my legs grow back after time
And I stare into my reflection
And place my glasses down
And I look into my eyes and shake my head
Bowed in honesty.
For in my eyes I see me
And in my eyes truth lies, and I know me
And you don't.

I shave my legs to no avail,
As the hairs grow back,
I look into my darkened soul and I weep,
For you, 'cause you look and gawp at my shell
For you who cannot and will not look into my eyes
And never see me and never open your arms
And shy away from internal embrace
You who'd never confront emotion, willingly.

I have no solutions and I wait and I try
And when I get tired of waiting, I shave my legs.

Hannah Miller

NIGHT CAT

(A dedication to my cat Jasmine.)

Slender black silk coat,
Gliding through the dark
Catching shadows,
Silent and secret.

Flash green eyes
Luminescent 'gainst the thick black night.
She stalks patiently, anticipating her prey
Heart thumping to the excitement of kill,
As mouse screams.

She slinks along the back yard walls,
Proud, vain -
Not the cat I know at all -
Living her other life
As I lay sleeping.
Morning dawns,
Sunlight casts lazy pattern through Nottingham lace.

She's on my pillow, purring.
Stretching luxuriously,
Yawns, pink mouth gaping.

Caressing her soft belly, I ask -

'Where have you been in the night?'

Little do I know . . .

Joanne Burrows

BROKEN PROMISES

You gave me a dream,
then you took it back.
You stole my heart,
then you watched it crack.

I gave you a dream,
for two to share.
I gave you my heart,
to show you I care.

We both made promises,
I thought they were clear.
We both had dreams,
I hoped were sincere.

Now that we're far apart,
I'm lost and alone.
We should be together,
for the world to see.

My heart, my dreams, my promises too,
always, forever, remain faithful to you.

Angela Dawn Phair

FATHER

I'd like to send this thought to you
It's taken from my heart.
You've always been there, when I needed you
In fact you've been there from the start.
You're a very special person
To do the things you do.
Your love and strength surround me
Your guidance helps me through.
I wish you all the happiness
That you've always given me.
You'll always be my hero
I want for you to see.
That just to say I love you
The words don't seem enough.
So I hope this message helps
For you to understand.
I may not say it often
But father you make me proud.

Rebbecca Byrom

EMPTINESS

I've tasted, a bit of life
Today's the day
I tasted, gold and spice
But come what may

There's something missing
you cannot tell
I smile and chatter
you cannot tell

At the back of my mind
there holds a story
My inward glory
has flown away

I'm not altogether sure
what it is
Maybe emotion, that I miss
Love?
Like cuddled up by the tele
A coffee cup, you see

Meaning warmth, acceptance
of being here
A cold flicker, of the heart
Something missing

Tracy Charters

The Dancing Bears

Dancing poses
Rings through their noses
Red hot plates to obey
Bears' sadness, bears' dismay
Once with their mothers
Now alone
In the circus, on their own
Claws snipped
Out come the teeth
The bears' pain is beyond belief
Day after day another show
Will their torture ever go?
Who in their right mind
Would want to see
These beautiful creatures
In agony?

Gillian Snipley

UNTITLED

Three score years and ten
is a good innings
Now your batting days are over
but you're still a member of the club

From the pavilion you see mistakes
that need not be.
If only they would listen to
a member of the club.

Four score years and seven
Take one step nearer to heaven

Batting, bowling or fielding
are out of the question but -
While ever you pay your subscription
you're still a member of the club.

From here, where? Who knows?
Decisions are made by the captain of the club

Elizabeth Brown

FROM A MOTHER TO A DAUGHTER

Would that I could heal you, make you whole again,
Undo the harm of passing years
And hold you in my arms as I did when you were small,
Soothe you, smooth you, kiss it better, see you laugh once more.
Would that I could tell you that I care
But I cannot seem to say the words.
They wait unformed, unframed by oyster lips
Though my heart feels like it's cracking from the strain.
But listen in the stillness of the night
And you will maybe sense the love I cannot speak,
Inchoate thought taking shape to arrow out to you,
My daughter, whom I laboured to bring forth.
So much misunderstanding has underscored our lives,
Unravelling the web of our relationship
And yet perhaps a tenuous thread maintains a frail connection
And we can weave the warp and weft to bring us close again
Until we hold each other as we did when you were small,
Tears mingling, joined in sorrow as we mourn your unborn child.

Jan Phoenix

HEAVY DUTY

Crash! Bang! Wallop!
The light had left us blind
We entered into a glittered room
The door was open wide

We were dressed in preparation
With jewellery heaven sent
Behind the glitter were the shadows
And so the ceremony went

'Get ready, take your places'
The room was very tense
As the ring slipped on my finger
He said 'Let the battle commence'

Two solitary soldiers
No boundaries yet drawn
We fought to find the limits
Our weapons, tongues of swords

Tongues were locked in battle
Once were locked in love
We dragged each other to our knees
Where we were forced to look above

There, I begged for His forgiveness
At last, I felt some peace
I let go of the anger
Then was helped from off my knees

He will take us in His hands now
To do with as He'll please
And in whatever form it takes
Will end our misery.

Kez

BEST FRIENDS

I feel peripheral
We used to be
best
friends
and now
we're not

Is this
what
being
grown-up
is?

I don't like it.

Mary Drayton

Falling Apart

I'm falling apart
I lost all that I had
Everyone's against me
It makes me so mad
Can't anyone see
How it's tearing me up inside
It's like me against the tide
I know that I can't win

I'm falling apart
I can't take it anymore
My heart is bruised and sore
Everything I do is wrong
It's so hard for me to be strong
My life's gone down the drain
I can't take all this pain

I'm falling apart
I should have known you'd break my heart
I should have known you'd make me cry
All I want to hear from you is why
Why won't you care?
I'm not asking a lot
I don't think I'm being unfair
I'm giving you all I've got

Amanda Steel

MY OLD WICKER CHAIR

I know I should take more exercise -
I would if I could
Find the time and the way
But I have been busy all day.
Although I know it would be wise
And healthy to exercise,
To tell you the truth I quite despair
For I'd rather sit in my old wicker chair.

I cleaned the windows, inside and out,
And polished the wood surround:
I swept the carpet, and then I found
A spider had woven its web around
The lamp shades, so these I dusted:
And then I saw the sun outdoors
And thought, 'I'll leave the household chores
Or this fine weather is wasted'.

I walked up and down mowing the lawn
And trimmed round the edges as well:
I weeded the border and when all was in order
My ankles began to swell.
I lifted potatoes and planted leeks,
And hoed round the onions with care:
I know I should exercise - I haven't for weeks -
But I slept in my old wicker chair.

N M Beddoes

Why

Nobody spoke to the
Pale faced child
She sat in the corner
She never cried
They didn't tell her
About sad or glad
Now she is older
And understands why
They couldn't tell her
Because they didn't
Cry
They never said
They loved me
I often wonder why
I never heard them
Laugh out loud
Or ever saw them cry
I wish they'd said
They loved me
I often wonder why
I love you
I miss you
I'm too shy to say
So for the time being
I will lock them away
As I get braver
I will shout out
Real loud
I love you
I love you
I've said it
Hooray!

Isobel Zilke

FRIENDSHIP

When all the world's against you
And all that you do, goes wrong
Your heart if full of sorrow
The days are much too long.
When no-one seems to have the time
To stop and talk awhile.
Remember that you have a friend
Who's ready with a smile.

When you feel you cannot cope
With life's hectic pace.
When your heart is heavy
And you want to hide your face.
Remember that you have a friend
Who understands your pain,
Who'll help you through the darkness
Into the light again.

When everything goes wrong for you
And troubles come your way,
When your mind's so weary
That you cannot even pray.
Remember that you have a friend
Who'll offer you their hand
When you feel you're falling,
A friend who'll help you stand.

D A Seagroatt

GIFT

Hush now baby
Tenderness springs forth
With all promise
The richness and newness of a fresh life

Hush now baby
Loved, nurtured, cherished
Pure beauty exuding from your eyes
Exuberant joy of being loved
Carry you through

Lift you up high
Treasured precious gift

Angela Kiley

The Animal Within!

Men, they're just like children
With a mental age of six
Except, instead of playing with their trains
They turn their minds to sex
'Honey, how are you feeling?'
And 'How's you headache now?'
What they really mean to say
Is, 'Can I get it now?'
It's like they want a sweetie
But you say 'Not before your lunch'
Then their faces trip them
And they go and get the humph!
You've to forget about the dishes
And forget the dinner too . . .
Leave the children at their nanna's
Running a house, they haven't a clue!
But then sometimes we must admit
That we need them after all
So strip off your apron, forget the chores
And pin him to the wall!

Lynn Harper

Sarcasm Of The Injured

Excuse me for being angry,
but I have no reason to apologise.
My feelings are sacred -
- and you have no reason to criticise.
I have been injured,
and you show no concern.
my welfare means nothing -
- I am but a number who follows your rules.
Excuse me for being angry;
you care nothing.
I have affections -
- I bruise easily.
But.
You are empty.
Devoid of emotion.
Who is superior?

Leigh Gillingham

THE HOLLOW HEART

You took your leave some time ago,
Or was it yesterday?
Time is but confusion
As I live from day to day.

For you the pain is over.
Though it still preys on my mind.
But I too must suffer
The pain you've left behind.

Birthdays, Christmas, Father's Day,
No cards bought to send.
Instead, the scent of flowers
With your ashes blend.

Death can cast a shadow,
Over all your hopes and dreams.
It swiftly brings a yearning
For all the 'might-have-beens'.

Resentment, hate and anger,
These I can't deny.
But it doesn't really matter
When we say goodbye.

Life, it must continue
And I have learned to cope.
Grief has now been replaced,
By fulfilment, strength and hope.

Grief is the pain we have to bear.
For loving one no longer there.
But the greatest pain that could befall
Would be never to love at all.

Jacqueline Gray

To Diana Our Beautiful Princess Our Queen Of Hearts

A handsome prince met a beautiful girl.
A nation watched as their love did unfurl.
They wed at St Paul's, a right royal affair.
How we rejoiced, they made a wonderful pair.

The girl now our princess, did the right thing.
Gave birth to two boys, one born to be king.
She melted our hearts, grew more beautiful each day.
We all thought so proudly, she'd be our queen one day.

But something went wrong, and they drifted apart.
Then came the divorce, which I'm sure broke her heart.
Our beautiful princess then travelled the world,
Showing compassion and kindness to the ill and the old.

The two little princes were her pride and joy,
She showered them with love, as they grew from baby to boy.
Each time she came home she'd open her arms wide,
And they would rush up so happy to be by her side.

Then came the day so terrible and tragic,
The light in her eyes, always sparkling and magic,
No more will sparkle no more will shine,
God took her from us, our princess devine.

Princes William and Harry, made us feel proud,
As they said goodbye to their mother, amid a vast crowd.
Diana we love them, just as we loved you,
Our beautiful princess, the world's princess too.

God bless Diana, you will be forever in our hearts.

Joyce Edmonds

LOVE FOR THE CHILDREN

Shadows of the past present themselves
a mother lost in pre-pubescent days.
The comfort of an age of innocence
lies in tatters while the mind tries
to traverse a mental maze.

Did my young life feel so very special?
Not much money, but we never went without
all the comfort, warmth, and love
cocooning us all as a family
of that we never were in any doubt.

So I wonder why all children
can't be loved the way that I was,
why must some endure rejection
others live in constant fear.
All the youngsters who are homeless,
perhaps we think it doesn't matter
should we all switch off and choose
to close our ears.

The sadness goes much deeper
lying heavy on my being,
it's the sight of so much pain
that leaves its mark.
There are children who are living
on the streets of every country
and where no one seems to care
these souls are groping in the dark.

So much pain in those young faces,
watching it I feel so helpless
just an onlooker who feels the need to cry,
In God's name what are we doing?
Hope one day we won't be asking,
why can't children all be loved the same as I.

Mary Hoy

DOLPHIN DAY

He rises from the waters deep
With an eternal and gentle smile
Eyes that shine with untold intelligence
And a call that is heard for many a mile.
Blue water drips from shining skin
As he frolics by moon and sun
His play is intent and always alert
For he treasures the life he has won.
He has saved the life of many a man
The same kind who seek to kill
They would end his life with violence
For the sake of their own weak will.
He has been abused and corrupted
Though his love is enduring and strong
He would lead a man to safety
That same man would do him wrong.
His nature is to care and love
Though he's hunted and driven away
He's determined to save the good in man
Till the dawn of the 'Dolphin Day'.

Siarah

THE JOURNEY

When a girl becomes a woman
She may leave a safe cocoon
That guarded and protected her
Just like inside her mother's womb

Now she treads the path of life
She enters the unknown
However will she handle it
She's waiting to be shown

Instinct - words of wisdom
Instilled in her through care
Will guide her on her journey
And help her to prepare

But armed with no experience
Her expectations may be high
Then when she hits reality
They're squashed - new rules apply

How will she mend her broken heart
Survive - move on - Mature
She - alone, - must find the answer
For no one's really sure

To help her they'll be lessons
No one else can bear her pain
For if they try to bail her out
A girl - she will remain

Pauline M Foran

THREE OLD MAIDS

Three old maids, why we don't know,
We go every week to the Darby and Joan,
But nobody offers to take us back home,
We'd like to go courting, fed up on our own,
We're three old maids.

Three old maids, why we don't know,
We don't mind if it's a Harry or Joe,
Just say the word, and we're raring to go,
So come along fellows oh don't be so slow,
We're three old maids.

Three old maids, why we don't know,
You've got to admit she's a very good cook.
I've tried every trick in the book,
She's done her best without any luck.
We're three old maids.

Three old maids, why we don't know,
Look us over, we've really got style,
Just to get hitched, we'd walk a few miles,
Our only aim, is to walk down the aisle,
We're three old maids.

I'm ready, I'm willing, and I'm free.

K Cleworth

Parched

I need some tender loving care
Do you have Phostrogen to spare?
My leaves are dry, I need a drink
I wonder if you ever think
That wives need nourishment as well
Or else they start to feel like hell,
Their roots begin to shrivel too
And then they don't know what to do.

You've got to fertilise each week
To keep things healthy, at their peak!
Then leaves will grow and flowers appear
And give you pleasure through the year,
Talk to your plant and it will strive
To do its very best to thrive
And with that tender loving care
You could end up with something rare.

Of course you can just throw away
A plant that's old and passed its day -
But really that's a waste of money
And wasting things just isn't funny
When you can cherish what you've got
Ready established in its pot,
Remember a plant is like a wife
Given love it springs to life!

Frances Henton

SINGLE

Not married yet dear people say
Still waiting for Mr Right to come
  your way,
We can't understand it cause
  you're not bad looking,
And you could always take a
  course in cleaning and cooking.

Think what you've missed not
  having a child,
Those little darlings all meek
  and mild,
And a man to come home to every night,
to love and comfort and hold you tight.

We think you've missed out cause
  it's not the norm
To be happy, single, and have a life
  of your own
A man is the answer to everything
It doesn't matter about a
  wedding ring.

I just smile sweetly
My answer's always the same,
I want a man with a strong will,
Made out in my name.

Christine Williams

Child Of Mine

The feelings start deep down in your tummy,
It often makes you come over all funny,
You place your hand upon your tum,
And worry about the size of your bum.

You soon start to develop a lump,
Which quickly turns into a round bump,
A kick in your side you feel today,
'Just feel here' to Daddy you say.

The veins in your legs soon start to swell,
The size of your breasts is getting hell.
Still it's worth it you say to each other at night,
But secretly wish your clothes weren't so tight.

So it's nine and a half months and you're overdue,
You still can't decide on white, pink or blue,
Playing the waiting game is hard enough,
Without varicose veins, feeling fat and rough.

'Stop pushing' the nurse says 'you'll just have to try,'
But I just want to curl up and cry,
The head is now out, not long left now,
As I call her a silly old cow.

Still the nurse doesn't mind, no she doesn't care,
Only smacking baby's bum for its first breath of air,
'It's a boy Miss Chadwick' she says with a smile,
As I sigh with relief, it's all been worthwhile.

Kimberley Chadwick

A Difficult Task?

Who needs a man - not me!
He passed the pepper when I asked for salt,
But of course typical man (it wasn't his fault!)
Then I requested - 'Walk the dog please love,'
So he made his way to the nearest pub.
I asked him once to iron a skirt,
He came down later with my dark blue shirt.
Ten years on and it had to end.
I said I'd still like to be his friend.
I flushed the marriage down the drain,
The silly man was driving me insane.
Any offers - I'm single again!

Barbara Lynch

I Loved You

I loved you and you never knew
As I looked into your eyes, it was as if I was looking into the very soul of you
So calm and strong, so firm and kind.

I loved you and you never knew
You see, I couldn't tell you
As someone else had already given their love to you
Yet despite knowing this my love still grew.
I was happy just being near to you.

I loved you and you never knew
And I know that forever in my heart,
I'll go on loving the bitter sweet memory of you.

N J Brocks

OH DO I ONLY WORK PART-TIME

The day starts off at six o'clock
when down the stairs I go
trying not to make a sound
I'm moving to and fro.
I get out all the breakfast things
and make packed lunches too,
sort out just what they need that day,
and now I want the loo.
Then while they're having breakfast
I'll lay their clothes in place,
and polish shoes, get school bags out,
for the bathroom, there's a race.
At half past eight, we're off to school
a bus ride and we're there,
and then I'm off to work myself
I'll miss them, cos I care.
At three o'clock I finish work
to school I go with speed.
Wondering what to make for tea,
a cuppa's what I need.
Then back into the house we go
they natter for their tea.
I'm washing up from breakfast time
then there's the laundry -
cooking, cleaning, washing clothes
listening to them read
telling bedtime stories
now is what they need.
At last now I can sit down
and try to watch TV
I close my eyes, then open them
'Oh no!' it's half past three.

Signed
A tired mum.

Chloé Brook

THE LOTTERY

I haven't won the lottery,
Why hasn't it been me,
I just want all six numbers,
Not the occasional three.

'20' that's my birth date,
Of September, that's month '9'
My bust, it measures '36'
I'll mark that on the line.

I bought a lottery keyring,
Six balls fall in the holes,
If I won the 'big one'
I could achieve my goals.

It's 8 o'clock on Saturday,
I switch the TV on,
Lancelot is mixing
All the balls up in the drum.

The first ball, number '20'
The second, number '9'
My heart is beating faster,
I down a glass of wine.

The final four have dropped now,
I blink, myopically,
I can't believe I've picked all six
On this week's lottery!

I hear alarm bells ringing,
A familiar melody,
It's Monday morning 8 am,
I'd dreamt my fantasy.

Louise D Andrew

Last Thoughts

She died tidily
Sheet folded back
On stark white counterpane.
Hands clasped before her
Tidily.
Each of us pigeon-holed
Labelled black or white
No untidy grey in-between.
Each fault filed
In neat rows.
In her tidy mind
Lapsed promises gnawed
At her love
Wearing it down to the bone.
Unkept visits to her
Dust-free rooms -
Absence of warmth
In our monthly 'Hallo's'
But she was 'mother'
And birth cords are strong
And, in that moment
When she lay peaceful - pale - and
Colder than life
I loved her.

Joan Miller

Growing Old

It's not very funny growing old,
You soon get tired, you soon get cold.

I have lots of friends,
But forget what they're called
The boys that I knew
Have all gone bald.

There's so many things,
You cannot remember
I don't know if it's May, June or September.

I'm off with my trolley
going shopping on Monday.
I get half way there and
find out it's Sunday.

Ten o'clock strikes, it's time for my bed
I've got on two jumpers
a woolly cap on my head.

I put in my curlers,
My teeth in the pot.
I wind up the cat and
put out the clock.

It's not too bad, if you smile
Have a joke, I'd have a cigarette, but I don't
know if I smoke.

M Meldrum

Free For All

I know what inspires me to write
It's the spirit of spring, putting winter to flight,
The new shoots on the barren bushes,
Songs of blackbirds, larks and thrushes,
All contribute to my joy
Pen and paper I must employ
And share Cornwall's beauty with all around
Heavenly sounds of nature abound
There's not a computer to be found,
That can compete or compare with the sound
Of waves crashing on the shore
And seagulls crying their call for more
As fishermen sail into the bay
And toss from their boat, the 'dish of the day'.
The seagulls a mass of moving white
Hovering ready for the flight
Preparing to descend for the fight
For fish, is sheer delight
It brightens up a cloudy day
And best of all there's nothing to pay.

Margaret Chambers

THIRD WORLD WOMAN

She wraps her Yorkshire blanket
around her bony shoulders
Hoping for a handout
of food from far off places.
Knowing news has been told
of all the starving races
Clutching tiny baby
knowing he was born to die
All she can do is love him
and shoo away the fly
Many miles she walked today
Just to gain some hope
She must beg for charity
Alone she cannot cope
The earth so dry from lack of rain
Crops won't grow this year
She bears the hunger pangs of pain
and hangs on to her life so dear
She hears a lone bird's anxious cry
and lives in hope of better days
The food is served, it's not good enough,
But quietly she gives her thanks
and wraps the Yorkshire blanket
around her bony shoulders
Sitting through the day
waiting for the night

E Heptinstall

MIRROR, MIRROR

I look in the mirror -
What do I see?
A face full of pimples
Staring at me!

My nose is lop-sided -
My lip sprouts a 'tash
And would you believe it
I've come out in a rash!

Why am I destined
To have such a clock
That looks like it's
Just been bashed in with a rock?

But with it I'm stuck
So I'd best not be sad
'Cos when I put on a smile
I'm not half as bad!

Liz Sitti

The Twilight Years

When all your kids have grown up
and granny is your name.
When time is not much on your side,
but hindsight is the game.

When shelves become too high or low
and policemen seem too young.
The years seem all too short
and the climb upstairs too long.

And now you need the big print books
and the wireless is preferred.
Why is it everyone whispers so?
It really is absurd.

You feel your life is useless
and coming to an end.
But then your children's children come
and drive you round the bend.

You reminisce with friends and peers,
to remember the good old days.
The bad times even seem less hard
and you laugh at people's funny ways.

It's all life's ups and downs you see,
that weaves this tangled web.
But if you had your time again,
there's naught you'd change or beg.

Jean Selmes

MEDIA GIRL

It's a media world
        with a media girl.
A media girl
        with tight little curls.
She poses where all can see her style
With legs that stretch
        for half a mile.
Slim in the way that all should be.
Open those eyes,
        look and see -
It's a uniform world -
        we should all look the same
With one shape and face
        with only one name.
Imagine a world where this were the case
Everyone walking in time,
        with one pace
No freedom to be . . .
Sounds more like a prison to me.

Cathy Bulley

Coffee

I'm as bitter as the coffee,
That sits within my cup,
Had enough of my life,
And all my rotten luck.
Where can I go now?
I've been everywhere,
On a rollercoaster of emotion,
Suffered tears of desperation,
Almost died from despair,
I've lived and loved a few times,
It never got me anywhere,
Got fed up with having hidings,
And finding other women's underwear,
So tired of having children,
For men that didn't care,
Other people's lives seem perfect,
God, you didn't make things very fair,
I think I'll drink more coffee,
So I can stare bitterly into my cup,
And wish that the Lord,
Would grant me better luck.

Elaine Hawkins

HELL HATH NO FURY

Hell hath no fury like a woman
Who is scornful of her married name,
When discovering that her husband
Has left the toilet seat up again!

Danni Kember

Guilt Trip

Why do we women feel guilty
When we have been abused
Battered and misused
We often blame ourselves
Was my skirt too short?
Was my smile too wide?
Did I mislead him to stray aside?

All these guilty questions we ask ourselves
And never blame those bastards
We forget to tell ourselves
That they are the ones with twisted minds
That led them to behave in ways unkind
And we shouldn't hide away in shells
but scream straight at them '*Go to Hell*'

Capella Page

Closed Doors

Doors open and doors close and you
Say you're tired
Of mopping the floor and cleaning
Windows, and locking
Doors behind you
But do you ever think of me?

I'm just behind you,
And the floor is slippy when
I walk, the windows have
Condensation and I can't see
Through the frosted glass,
And every time I reach a door
It's locked. Shut.

I'm left behind you
In a box with no way out
And no light coming in, and the
Floor is slippy when I try to walk
Around my little space.

Gail Vernon

LINE DANCERS

They can't wait to get to class!
To hear again that upbeat country sound,
and join the lines of dancers
learning to stomp to fun routines,
With names like *Alley Cat* and *Cowboy Strut.*

When they dance in different lines,
the man drops back to watch his wife,
watch how quickly she learns the steps,
can improvise, yet keep the beat:
dancing her strong joy.

And because he feels unburdened
of his need to make her happy,
he warms to her.

And because she feels unhindered
by his many fumbled steps,
she warms to him.

When they pull on
their winter coats of compromise
to make the journey home,
both wish this latest craze
could last for ever.

Di Garstang

Deserted

After twenty five years you got up and went
You left me alone, the money all spent
Followed by all the hardship and tears
You treated me badly those last few years

You always said you would do this to me
When the children were gone, you wanted to be free
I never really believed that you would
So I stayed in the marriage as I thought I should

I will never understand the reason why
With three children grown up, time passing us by
When some of that time, should have been ours
To go for a walk or even look at the stars

To do some of the things we could never do
I only wanted to spend a little time with you
Your career came first all of your life
Was it too much to ask to spend some time with your wife?

Annette E Walker

IGNORED

Don't put me first.
I might die of shock.
Don't put my feelings before others,
I wouldn't know which way to look.
I'm being sarcastic, of course,
It's just that I'm feeling alone.
It's hard to be on the outside,
Living my life on my own.

Anna King

A Woman's World

Your ring of ownership weighs me down,
You say you're the king, so where's your crown?
You say I'm just your baby machine
Well your crown doesn't fit, Mr King
Every time I step outside,
You make me feel like I should be terrified,
Just your little girl who has to hold your hand,
Well, back off, because I'm the queen of this land!

This is a woman's world,
Where we don't have our hair curled just for you,
This is a woman's world,
Where we don't long to be held by you.

Well, just sit me down there,
So every man can sit and stare,
Incapable of going out to work,
But always the boss's perk,
Guess what, we're not going to take it anymore,
We're sick and tired of mopping your floor,
There're better things boiling away in us,
You'll learn - When's the next bus?

To a woman's world,
Where we don't get our hair curled just for you,
This is a woman's world,
Where we don't need to be held by you.

Lorraine Scutt (17)

Housewife's Lament

Somebody has to do the jobs
    That nobody else will do;
Somebody has to clean the bath,
    The sink, and even the loo;
Somebody has to wash the clothes,
    And iron them when they're done;
Somebody has to vacuum and polish,
    And cook for everyone.
Somebody has to make the beds,
    And change them when they need it;
Somebody has to walk the dog,
    Clean up its mess, and feed it.
Somebody has to shine the mirrors,
    And all the windows too;
Somebody has to decorate,
    And clean the house right through.
Somebody has to tidy up
    And clear away the mess;
Somebody has to do it -
    And somebody's me, I guess!

Pauline Hepple

Ladies Of A Certain Age

They used to meet on the third floor of department stores
in nameless seaside towns
swapping gossip and ailments in low innuendo
across the napiery
stirring potions in teapots
powdering away blushes and drawing comfort from teacakes
after the surgical nip and tuck
while the gliding models paused to display the latest in casual day-wear

Now the burn your bra generation has come of age
rewriting mid-life and celebrating cronage
now it's support groups and HRT
or women against HRT and that herbal cream you get from Ireland
to fan the flame of a vanishing libido
or douse the rosemadder rage rushing up to your throat
exercising pelvic floor muscles
when the knicker elastic's gone in your genitals and you've
forgotten why.
Now where was I?
'Sorry, I've gone spaghetti brained again,' gets a laugh these days
anti-ageism demands full dedication
libido and stamina enhancement supplementation
step aerobics, ginseng sandwiches and wild yam risotto for tea
fifty-five and she still runs ten orgasms round the block
before the executive board-meeting.

But the mourning lingers in the silence
too late for children now, too late for any more
when ageing and sagging doesn't seem quite so attractive
when a spreading waist and the feeling
of being dragged to a downhill future
withdraws you into a bow-headed wisdom of acceptance
as the body takes its toll against the wishes of the mind.

Rachael Clyne

Choosing a Hat

I thought I would buy a new hat today
To wear with my new summer clothes,
So I went along to the milliner's shop
With my very best friend, name of Rose.

Hats of every description were on show,
Splendid finery, such an array,
All decked with flowers, feathers and bows
A truly magnificent display.

Should I choose a cute little number,
Or one with a very large brim?
The assistant suggested I try one
With exotic fruits for the trim.

For approval I looked round for Rosie
But nowhere was she to be found,
It was then I heard the loud giggles
In fits of mirth, she was rolling around.

Next I tried on a large brimmed hat
Bedecked with feathers and bows,
But being too large, it dropped down o'er my eyes
And the feathers were tickling my nose.

Rose asked me to try a pretty pink hat
With a veil, flowers and lace
But the veil got caught up on my glasses
Sent them crashing to the floor from my face.

In the end I chose a plain little boater
But when the assistant told me the price
I thought I would just wear my hair after all,
You see my wig was equally as nice!

Barbara Sowden

A LIFE LESS MEANING

There are certain things in this life
That have no meaning.
If you get my meaning.
Sometimes things are meant to just be meaningless.
And no matter how far you dig, they have no hidden meaning,
No hidden depth.
And there is no subtext,
No metaphor,
In what I say next.
The true meaning of life is;
That everything is meaningless.

Rachel C Zaino

Trying, But What For What?

(Written by J Keel for J G)

No matter how hard you seem to try
You can make me laugh, you can make me cry!
I try to understand your ways, and your needs
A brand new experience, growing from seeds

My patience, my emotions, you'll change so fast
One day it's fine, the next it can't last
Just one more try, because I really do care
Ignoring your priority, but it's always there!

Knowing without words, it's not very kind
Consequences, kept to the back of your mind
One extra for you, a part you are missing
Just physical contact, hardly ever kissing

Clever , intelligent, street-wise or not
Feeling used is degrading, believe it or not
It was never my style, to give my heart without trust
But loving to make love, never just for lust

Only I feel like I do, but still it's my pride
Days turn to weeks, you're never by my side
Stone eventually crumbles, and so can my heart
Is it time to face reality, knowing we should part?

J Keel

She Glows

What happened to the girl I once knew?
No cares, all dreams, full of vigour
A smile so bright, sparkling eyes
Long, skinny legs, boy-like figure

At what point did she change
From a girl to a woman?
Who took away those gifts she was given?
Replaced with a foresight beyond her years
Yesterday's hopes turning to fears

The children, they came,
They grew up, they went,
The love of her husband she embraces,
Content,
For time has been kind,
She has love in her heart,
Blessings awarded, right from the start.

She picks up a mirror, she gazes deep,
When did she change? Looks lost in her sleep?
She smiles her warm smile,
For deep down she knows
She is loved, she is treasured
And on that thought, she glows.

Caroline Kinnear

WHY CHOOSE A TUBA?

I thought that the fiddle
Would be a real doddle
But my teacher said 'Screeches
Are the worst of your features.
Your tunes and your scales
Are like desolate wails.
The oboe has no bow -
Please give it a go.' So

I did but I found
That I made a weird sound
Had a hitch with the pitch;
Was a weed with the reed.
The thought of a solo
Would make me feel so low
I'd rather be dead.
'Til somebody said
'Why not choose a tuba?

It's big and it's brassy!
It's sassy! It's classy!
With every loud oompah
You know that you'll boom far!'
Now the outlook is grand -
I'm the star of the band!
I *did* choose the tuba.
Would you?

Freda Eyden

DREAMS

I must have been preoccupied
With my mother's need for things
Like soap and elastic. Because
At night I would think,
Concentrate and dream of these.
My efforts were unrewarded,
My endeavours unsuccessful,
My laden arms were empty
At the light of day.

Sometimes I was selfish:
I thought of things I wanted.
Possession of glasses
Was my aim
To be the same -
Everyone in the family wore them.
Again I failed.
But the practice had its benefits:
I learned to control my dreams.

Kate Sumner

Out Of The Kiln

When I did not know, Your name,
You knew mine.
When I, could not have dreamed
Of your existence,
You had mapped out mine.
In beds of roses, we smell,
The sweet perfume of life,
Failing to understand, the cruelty
Of the thorns.
Dismembering heart and soul,
Impersonators in loco parentis.
Tarantualaic webs of deceit,
Like blankets, softly smothering,
Cries of misuse.
Your tears poured, into the broken pot.
Bathing it so often . . .
Softening the cracked earth,
Gently remoulding your child.
And today, I have seen through your eyes,
Master potter . . .
You, are my Father.

Jacquie L Smith

GOODBYE

Your lies can't hurt me any more
I won't look back as I close the door
You'll never fill my heart with pain
Or hold me in my arms again.

You have turned away from me so many times
What sin was I guilty of, what was my crime?
You never ask how I feel
This life we are living is unreal.

You hurt me with the words you say
And make me cry every day
You've made me feel that I was in the wrong
Out of place and didn't belong.

You made me cry a million tears
Filled my heart and soul with fears
You destroyed my love in so many ways
And filled me with sadness every single day.

No, you won't hurt me any more
I've left for good and closed the door
You'll never see me cry
'Cos I've left without saying goodbye.

Cathie Mullen

My Love Is Like A Rotary Machine Gun

I'm his it seems, or so they say
Defined, categorised and locked away.
Only a fraction of the whole
Incomplete, without a soul

So as a woman goes through life.
She finds a husband, becomes a wife,
She has her children by the score
And sometimes wonders if there's more

We women are such fragile things,
Earthbound angels without wings.
Or else dependant on the talk
A kind of demon with pitchfork

So weak, so feeble, less than one.
Pass the acid, load the gun.
I'll strike a blow for womankind
And prove we hold the ties that bind.

Violence is not a male domain,
Yes, it's true, I can cause pain.
More likely warrior that a nurse
Slow to sweet talk, swift to curse.

Beware my sex for we fight back,
Our brains make up for strength we lack,
And modern weapons are designed
To be light weight and more refined.

So, careful, when you stoop too low,
Say that harsh word, strike that blow.
Around the corner straight from heaven,
An avenging *AK47!*

Philippa Driscoll

Within The Mind Of The Estranged Wife

Deep and bitter pain,
Cut as with jagged edges,
Of a shattered mirror's glass,
Image once seen,
Lies amidst the ruined fragments,
This perfection of the whole,
Then by chance,
A dream into a nightmare turned.

Seldom stopping,
Now into its corridors I race,
No turning back,
Yet no way out,
Trapped within this room,
With doors and windows locked,
The only sound is in the mind,
I feel the beating heart.

As panic grips the throat,
And muscles tight contract,
Then, once more, a blur,
As tears fall,
Cower in a corner,
Dab the red sore eyes,
As loud and clear his voice rings out,
With empty promises once more.

Ann G Wallace

Running Mascara

Coffee with salt from the tears in my eyes.
You said you were working late, but I see through your lies.
Eggs over easy and we carry on as before.
You still kiss me goodbye as you rush through the door.
Rings on your fingers, no bells on your toes,
A wife and a child, but who cares about those?
Just more running mascara
Washing the pots as you drive down the street.
You say you have a meeting but I know just who you're going to meet.
I make the dinner as the day turns to night.
I want to get this sorted out, but I don't want to fight.
Ring on your finger, no bells on your toes.
He shall cause tears wherever he goes.
More running mascara
Apologies come as you walk through the door.
We don't say anything, just go on like before.
Coffee with salt and breakfast with lies.
Big black salty tears fall unnoticed from my eyes.
Just more running mascara

Helen Satchwell

EVOLVING

We may have grown up together
Yet there was so much
He didn't know about me
So much I wanted to disclose
But was unable to
I had to hold back
He watched me evolve
From a shy, reserved young girl
Into what I represent
Into what I am today
He doesn't want me of yesterday
Me of yesterday is me of today

Kauser Parveen

Loss

Empty as fog,
The sky hung grey,
As rain poured and seeped,
And ran like teardrops on the panes,

Misting the green hills,
Like smudged charcoal,
As through wistful lanes,
An aching wind searched emotional,

Landscapes.
A year has passed,
Lost,
As empty minds.

Rosaleen Higgins

Some Hope! (Or Shirley Valentine's Clone)

I wonder why I cradle dreams
of candles lit in sultry scenes
hibiscus awnings, palmy trysts
our glasses twined in champers' kissed
while soft sea breezes lap and beat
Calypso rhythms round our feet?

When in reality it's dawn
the day is dull, the drapes are torn
the tea's unmade and cat wants out
The postman knocks, the offspring shout
and dishes groan in grease gone cold
and I feel grey and fat and old.

Perhaps I'll win the pools one day
be slim and sleek and flit away
and leave them all to sort things out
to wash their clothes and peel the sprouts
to shop and iron, clean and weed
and call themselves to school and feed.

While I in blazing balm will bask
oblivious of each mundane task
with time to ponder thoughts profound
to sing and dance and swan around
in flowing garments, fancy free
and even pen a poesie!

Rosemary Keith

My Grandad

A man so very warm and alive within each space,
with a smile as warm as a summer's day.
and a gleam that touched his face.

A tolerance beset him,
with a laugh as deep as any sea,
Why did death kiss this man,
so alive and free?

He'd yawn with humour upon his lips,
and dig with nature at his side,
his sleeves rolled up, as they always were,
his armour was his pride.

On an autumn day, he'd hit the ground
with a walking stick he bore,
and search for chestnuts in the dew,
with that winning smile he wore.

He opened up a world for me,
the universe with all its stars,
we'd sit and count them one by one,
from Jupiter to Mars.

Now grown up, I recall these moments
full of pleasure,
and with every beat of my heart,
his memory I will treasure.

Nancy Smith

THE CHILDREN OF DESPAIR

A neo naked man child insane inside his own personal power struggle
Reaches for a small, seemingly insignificant button.
Screeching alarms of absurd finality echo round the world.
The concept of time disintegrates into an abyss of infinite
Nothingness and man's inhumanity to man becomes reality.
Forcibly ejaculated screams of terror rise in a thousand million throats.

A thousand million mothers
Cry a thousand million tears
A thousand million fathers
Comfort the mothers of the children of despair.

D Sinclair

MIRROR MIRROR

Mirror mirror on the wall,
Twice as wide and half as tall,
With your wicked light define,
Crease and flaw and scar and line,
Magnify me; insecure,
Frizzy hair and open pore.
Tell me, is that cellulite or just a trick?
Quicksilver fright.
On the wall you proudly hang
Staring at me, old and young
Scrutinising every beauty
On her quest of youthful duty,
Will she pass the strict inspection:-
Frightened of her own reflection
You repel me and allure me.
Terrorise and ostracise me
Who's the gawky girl I see
Gazing at me warily?
Overgrown and out of place
Bulbous nose and crooked face

Helen Bailey

Bye

She was strong with will decisive
Fool scorned with words derisive

Set apart her strength her guide
Opines expressed afraid a mind

Compassion there but rarely known
Few aware it could be shown

Were you stricken by her wrath
Ne'er again you'd cross her path

Hidden perhaps behind the pride
Sharing life had she once cried

Had there been a hurt a pain
Resolve to never feel again

Passage into solitary years
Despite facade were there fears

Her love was without reserve
For feline bodies every curve

Nostalgia raises doubt some shame
Was she a broken daisy chain

She loved me as her protégé
I didn't care my feet were clay

Sad remorse has come too late
For Bye, I was a twist of fate.

Muriel Crook

A Happy Gran

Looking back over the years,
At the age of seventy five
I find I've shed very few tears
And it's great to be alive
From early days I was spoiled rotten,
By Mum, and Dad and sister too.
Happy days never forgotten
All days sunny, all skies blue.

Teenage worries not for me
We all toed the line, you see.
No drugs, graffiti, or furtive sex
The shame of these kept us in check.

At seventeen we were at war -
Survival chances very slim
So many men returned no more
But mine did and I married him.

We had two boys now fully grown
And grandchildren to bless our days
And best of all, a happy home.

I smile and think of all the days
When skies were blue and laughs were many
The dark days? . . . Were there any?

Doris M Ilkin

It's A Woman's World

It's a woman's world - Well of course it is!
Whatever she's got soon becomes his!
'What's yours is mine, and what's mine's my own!'
Many a true word in jest is sown
A life free from worry, trouble and strife
If only you agree to become his wife
'Just bring up the kids and keep the house clean'
Surely this is the height of every girl's dream?
And when he gets home from a hard day at work
You run to the door - now don't you dare smirk!
With a smile on your lips and done up to the nines
You say 'Dinner is ready - just uncork the wine!'
When the children start school - Oh what a doddle!
You can get part time work without any trouble
Then juggle the housework, the kids and the job
And still look as though it's really 'No prob!'
And when your poor man's not feeling well
Although it's a cold, he's feeling like hell
You pamper and spoil him and act like a mother
When he bangs on the floor, you'd like him to smother
You sweetly call, 'I'll be up in a minute'
If there was a medal for patience you'd definitely win it!
But all in all, mine's not all that bad
He's kind and considerate, and a terrific dad
And he does have his uses - some are quite nice
Like for warming my feet when they are feeling like ice!
For catching the spiders that crawl round the room
And holding my hand as we gaze at the moon
So even on days when I'm feeling quite harried
I'll never regret the day we got married

Jennifer Kinghorn

THE PEACOCK

Oh peacock you remind me so
of someone close I used to know
whose strutting walk and princely stance
would leave my pulses all askance

And how I loved that confidence
that surety, what second sense
how you were never, never wrong
and how you knew it all along

You didn't know what I could do
if I should separate from you
your wisdom saw me through the day
your humour wonderful, you'd say

Oh bird with all your clarity
why can't you see I must be me
and though I leave you cock-a-hoop
it's time the peahen flew the coop

Evelyn Durham

Ever Since . . .

Ever since I was a little girl
I had a dream I wanted to fulfil,
Now you may find it funny, you may even laugh,
But most of all, I bet you'll find it daft,
But still I'll plough ahead,
Just listen to what I haven't said,
When I was a wee little munchkin.
Sitting on my dear pop's lap reading,
He used to read me many fairy tales,
But there was something I couldn't understand,
The heroes were always males,
And the princesses, whilst blonde and beautiful,
Were, how shall I phrase it, docile and respectable,
Now there's something I have to confess,
It really irritates me to see them so weak and helpless,
Whilst the men search for dragons to slay,
All women seem to do is chat and sew all day,
Now I'm not saying that's all bad,
But what really makes me mad.
Is that inside our delicate heads,
And brains that could rival the feds,
Now I'm not saying I want to be in the FBI
Or start a new life career as an international spy,
All I'm saying girls, is that we can be anything if we only just try.

Rowshownara Miah (16)

WOMEN'S FIB

It is good to see
a woman is no longer a horse
to be broken in and brought to heel
like a well-trained pup
the days are gone when we as women
were expected to marry as a duty
and those with no beauty became maiden aunts
yes, it is good to see
that a woman has the right to wear the pants
and no longer has to be escorted through the streets
by a man

The end of a girl's modesty
came late
it took till the twentieth-century
for man to rise, unwilling, to the bait
as the Pankhurst skirts were gathered in
ironically, a horse, belonging to the king
was to change the tide for women to win

And as I stand with my hands
immersed in the sink
the next millennium not a blink away
it seems the years since nineteen-thirteen
have shrunk into a single day

Julie Ashpool

Playing The Game

I do not like this spotlight
but if I cannot be seen there will be
no jam on their bread tomorrow.

Smile, never mind the draught
icing up your suspenders making you
wish for thermal knickers.

I should have got an education,
listened to the advice, but at sixteen
it never seems important.

A kiss behind the bike shed
is more exciting. By the time you wise-up
it's too late, and innocent eyes have to be fed.

I wonder where he is now,
as if I cared. My children will thrive,
he can go to hell.

Hand on your hip woman, chin up,
you are about to get in
out of the cold.

Keep talking, it's only a game,
and you will be tucked up in a warm bed
on your own, by midnight.

Eleanor West

Female Logic

Go on, spoil yourself.
You deserve it!
Forget about the spots you'll get on your chin.
Never mind about the inch you'll put on your waist.
You've worked hard.
Give yourself a treat!

Ugh! Just look at me.
Do I deserve this?
Why me? Why such rotten skin?
Just look at my waist-line. -
But, I do work hard,
I'll give myself a treat.

Barbara J Pimblett

If Women Ruled

If women ruled the world,
Would anything really change?
Would there be less disease
Would people feel less pain?

We strived so long for equality
But just how *equal* are we?
Women, like men want careers now,
This comes first before family.

Now don't get me wrong,
I'm not saying, we should go back to Victorian ways,
But did anyone stop and think about morals,
One's were losing in so many ways?

The rise in teenage pregnancy,
Many children have sex before they're fifteen,
The amount of feminine violence,
Girl gang are now frequently seen.

Women have changed and evolved,
But is it in the best way.
In our struggle for our freedom,
We threw a lot of our femininity away.

Would things change so much if we ruled?
I don't believe that would be true,
One can't rule over the other,
For things to change we have to unite,
Man and woman, me and you.

Leánne Broughton

HEART GIFTS

Many times in my day
I've tried to chase your memory far away
And banish you from my mind.
But, there to my surprise, amid my dreams as I sleep, it's you I find.

You bring such hope, such joy, such love to my heart like
I have never known.
And so for just a little while I no longer feel quite so alone.
But when I awake to find you gone, I'm only left with fear
For I can no longer hold you close and feel you near.

I know in my mind that you can never be mine in reality
But my heart will not listen to such common-sense and sanity.
How will I ever find peace when my heart and mind are so opposed
One saying, 'Stay,' while the other is saying, 'Go.'

But though you have gone,
A part of you still lives on.
It lives on in my heart
Where it refuses to depart.

There it glistens and shines with such beauty to beguile
That to my face it can't help but bring a smile.
I tell my heart that it's no good
But it won't listen to what it should.

It whispers softly to my mind
To seek and I will find
That hope and joy are the fruits of love that should be treasured
And are heart gifts beyond measure.

And so my mind finally surrenders to my heart
To try to seek my part.
I stop, I listen, then I say,
'Yes, this person is here to stay.'

'Okay heart, let's make a deal,
Let's stop fighting and start to heal.'

Jacqueline Barclay

TEN YEARS

Where have the last ten years gone
Yesterday should seem so long
Since I had that child of almost the same
The unfolding years for her still a game.

Which ten years of life would I chose as best
Or alternatively which ten would I detest
On the whole each has relevant value
Their keeping qualities one could argue.

Ten years of looks fading and looks to be kept
Each shadowed wrinkle is how long I have slept
Garden tilling and house toiling till my anger is boiling
Spoken words left untidied loved ones' lives soiling.

But what of the future ten years of life
Filtered sunlight, increased rain troubles rife
There are answers in pleasures and a wild abandon
Using my frontal mind forehead
With some kind of candour.

The splendour of conjuring life for a further ten years
Must in all certainty help allay some fears
Long ways are for continuing and not only coming
For after ten years there is another decade looming.

Margaret M Cassidy

Tomorrow

Tomorrow I'll see you
So today doesn't really matter
Tomorrow I'll hear you
So today lasts long
Tomorrow I'll laugh with you
And you'll be locked in my mind
Tomorrow I'll stand by you
But you will be blind
Blind to my senses
So I'll live for tomorrow
And today will last long.

Lynn Jean Barry

DIGITALLY PERFECT

My bathroom scales seemed past their day
Old they were, not much longer to stay
I'd been slimming, to lose some extra pounds
So heavy, I was, they made creaking sounds!

For over a month, the scales had read
The very same weight, though I'd underfed
No good were these, if I were to keep a tab
On the progress I was making, losing the flab!

So I treated myself to the best scales indeed
Top of the range, accuracy guaranteed
Digitally perfect, I could be well assured
They would truthfully tell how well I'd scored!

But my new scales were to give me an almighty shock
The very first time, it was as if they did mock
Registering the same old weight, my ego to dent
The only pounds lost were those I had spent!

Mary Wood

Prisoner

All her life she lived above the shop
on the main street of a drowsy little town.
In old age she lived in one room half-way up.
The bathroom, of course, was at the very top.
To reach the kitchen she'd plod slowly down
a spiral staircase to the narrow hall,
frail hand clinging to a silken rope along the wall.

Her room was long and gloomy with a list -
to port or starboard I could not have said -
a heavy wardrobe and a linen chest,
a two-bar fire to sit by while she dressed,
an antique sofa and a divan bed,
and all her life my aunt remained unwed.

I thought it was from choice until she showed
a faded photo of a handsome chap
and told me that he used to be her beau
until her father died at forty-two
and she was left behind to mind the shop.
'I could have been married to that man,' she said,
'but mother spent her widowhood in bed.'

And so for fifty years she stood instead
between the counter and the rows of labelled drawers
dolling out pills and potions green and red -
curlers and cough cures, penicillin, M and B's,
potassium permanganate and manganese,
prescriptions, purgatives and throat pastilles,
and smiling always at the customers.
'Good morning, dear, and how are you today?
I'll have this made up for you right away' -
A prisoner, conscious of her fading beauty
as daughter-like she strove to do her duty.

Jill McKenna

FEMME FATALE

I am the enemy, the wrecker of lives.
Caught up in the chocolate-box world of my mind
I was lost in the moment.
Swept along by the current
To drown in Avernus.
My senses abandoned
I dived deeper in.
Further I floated and could not turn back.
I clasped at her life and wrenched it towards me.
Shattered her dreams, her hopes and desires.
Blackened her trust and murdered her pride.
I took from her through mindless distraction.
I took from her.
Yet I did not want.
A thing to be discarded,
Thrown away.
Alone with my conscience
We battle to death.
Remorse is my jury
And guilt is my noose.

Ann-Marie Johnson

Dialogue With A Daughter

Daughter: In my teens I hated you,
And loathed your wretched rules.
'Home by twelve'. You should've known
my friends and I weren't fools.

Mother: But darling, there was danger.
Those skirts high on your thighs!
Mascara painted drag-queen thick
Around those gorgeous eyes!

Daughter: OK, but I was with a crowd.
I never was alone.
Yes mum, I should more often
Have called you on the phone.

Mother: Too bloody right! *Now, honesty!*
At times *I* felt hate too.
Searching streets at midnight
For a sight of you.

There never was. Trudge home. Half-mad,
Lie down, with every light on.
Brain on fire with thoughts of you
Spaced-out in bars in Brighton!

A woman's world, my once-wild child,
is a maelstrom of emotion.
A moody mess of violent hates,
Of family devotion.
You're now full-grown. I'm sixty-plus.
Today I feel we're friends.
May all our words have kind intent,
And our stories happy ends . . .

Elizabeth Mark

A Friend

You don't always need to see me,
To know that I'm your friend,
I just want you to know
On me you can depend,
When tears fill your sad eyes,
And the hurt won't go away,
When you need someone to share it with
You only have to say,
A friend's someone who's always there,
In good times and the bad,
They bring back all the memories,
Some happy and some sad,
No matter how long or whatever may fall
I'll always be there, waiting for your call.

Lilian Summers

ME, THE GREAT FEMINIST

I'm the great feminist,
I don't take any crap.
It's sexist pigs for dinner,
And I always wear a cap.
No way am I a housewife,
Or devoted to a man.
I treat men as inferior sex,
As only a woman can.
I go to all the protests,
And march around for hours.
I'm devoted to my society,
Rain, hail or showers.
I'll be a woman in power,
And show those sexist men.
That I the great feminist,
Can do the work of ten men!
And so I end my little rhyme,
Of those men causing strife.
I won't stand for it anymore -
It's great having a feminist's life!

Laura Cation

Images In Concrete

Spring gave me some moments
spilt from her arms: spilling
me on a summer place. A tunnel
curves out time, entwines my hair
on hedgerows - busy bundles of small
fingers free and - upturned bicycle
wheels spin grass verges, tumbling,
tumbling, tumbling delicately in all the sweetness
that we need, now . . .
Rushing vehicles muffle the
laughter; crack hard the
mellow fall, on a level that
won't now yield to my touch,
won't fill me with a warmth,
like nests and birdsong
swallowed in concrete flyovers,
solid bedrock of bridges.
And if my being here
could alter this, in dark wintry
underpasses, where trash now
blows on my wild youth, where
the hedgerows fail to blossom:
beside the derelicts I would lay
and let my ageing blood skirmish
while I rage - what fault is
this? Whose fault? Whose wish?

Marion Cummiskey

UNTITLED

(Dedicated to Lee Davey)

A part of me died today
A star fell from the sky,
Many questions left unanswered
Many answers question why?

Something in me died today,
Something precious, newly found,
A death, no more present in us
As if buried in the ground.

Part of my life died today,
Leaving a world of doubt
Part of me that disappeared
That I can't live without.

Life became incomplete today
Took a step into the past
A death which only two can sense
Enemies to the last?

Something lost its life today
The clouds shed tears of rain,
A piercing feeling in the heart
A never-ending pain.

Something in us died today,
A something ceased to be.
Two parts of a whole torn apart
Splitting the *us* and *we*.

Something in me died today
Loneliness appeared again
A part of you was lost today
Only in memory now to remain.

Laura Hofton

MODEL DREAM

Long thin brows
Dark lashes to the tips
Tiny pale nose,
Deep dark lips.

Beautiful blue eyes,
Set off her face,
There's no substitution
This queen you could not replace.

Her tiny waist,
All her bendy curves,
As she struts her stuff,
The catwalk she serves.

The cameras flash
She'll be on the front cover of all the top magazines.
If only I could look like her
You are my model dream.

Gemma Fryer

WEDDED MISS

We dined on limes
For most of our married life
Not the bowl of cherries
I supposed.
We slept on rusty bed springs
Instead of the bed of roses
I expected.
You wrapped me in barbed wire
Rather than a blanket
Of protection.
We trod on broken glass
Instead of following
The yellow brick road
To the end of the rainbow.

Sandra E Davies

LOVE'S FINALITY

When I needed you, longed for you,
You rejected my love, turning from me.
How desperately I clung, to false hope,
Finally realising, you had died within.
Love, once so vibrant and all consuming,
Enveloped us, in its loving folds,
Time stood still, as we reached dizzy heights.
Such intensity of passion, now dulled and tarnished,
What caused the chasm of our parting?
Were we blind, to the estrangement, between us?
When love's fire, becomes, mere dying embers,
Can a spark, once more, rekindle the flame?
Too late! My heart also is now frozen over,
No longer needing you, or desiring you.
Truly our love has faded, reaching its . . . finality.

Yvonne Charles

Canaries Were Singing In Cages

Mother can you hear me
Are your eyes shuttered blinds?
Unseeing these freesias their scent lost
In the wild tangled garden of your mind.
Drip-fed, disembodied
Can't you speak, squeeze my hand?

You lie humped in blankets
Listless, unaware
Yawning, blinking, semi-consciousness
Slumped in sleep disordered darkness
Whilst outside tall irises
Cast long purple shadows on the pond.

Still beds and hushed old ladies
Curtains billowing across the room
Her bed by the open window
Cool and calm
In the heat of June.

And canaries were singing in cages
Their song lilting through the air
As she lay dying and spoke
My name again and again
Saying goodbye.

The house seemed to be darkly mourning
Her life lay everywhere
Unfinished knitting, skeins of silk thread,
Blue mohair rug on the chair.

I put her silver thimble on my finger
And played the carved musical box
Back at her knee a child again
Crying for all I had lost.

Jan Ingram McCaffery

REJECTION

When we married you promised to love me,
Forever till death do us part,
Was it really so hard to keep that vow?
So easy to break my heart?

All the caring, all the sharing for twenty-two years,
All the memories happy and sad,
They don't seem to mean very much to you now,
Was your life with me really so bad?

I bore you three children, I cared for your home,
I supported your Army career,
And my reward for all this devotion and love?
Only rejection and tears.

So you've found someone new, does it give you the right,
To trade me in like last year's car?
Now that you've got a new model, is it really all over?
Have we really come that far?

I know I am angry and hurting right now,
And there's nothing at all I can do,
But the saddest part of all this mess,
Is that I'm still in love with you.

I've travelled the world as an Army wife,
It's all the life I have known,
So how can I start all over again,
When all that I lived for has gone?

Elizabeth M McNally

A Woman's World

Goodbye darling
He says as he goes
Out of the door
Leaving you, wondering
As never before.

You look in the mirror
And say why, oh why?
The woman I see
Is not like she used to be.

I dash here and there,
Coping, I certainly do,
My time is my own,
But gosh it's half-past-two.
He will be home for lunch,

Nothing prepared, dash it!
He will have to make do,
While I'm having mine at the Waldoff,
Then a make-over at Nancy's
It's goodbye darling to you.

I Oates

WOMEN

Women's work is never done
Especially, if you are a mum.
Clean the house!
Shop until you drop
Provide tasty meals,
Iron the clothes, after the wash.
Christmas, write the cards,
wrap the gifts,
Iron, *that dress* for her special date
meet the boyfriend
she thinks he's great!
And his new girlfriend
he thinks she's a dream!
He's shampooed his hair
and pressed his pants
even, take her to a dance.
We watch them, until they've grown
then they fly away, from home.
Leaving you and hubby on your own
so you tidy the garden, feed the dog,
take a walk, alone
And wish, they hadn't grown.
When they were young
they made a mess!
Now they've grown, you're on your own
And wish those youngsters
were small once more!

Irene G Corbett

Grandma

Grandma wears old-fashioned clothes,
Specs perched on the tip of her nose,
Shining eyes and wrinkled face,
Pensive, walks at her own pace.
Frowns at strangers to her door,
Waves to those she's seen before!
Frail form with strength of two -
Always has so much to do!
Flicks the dust off rocking chair
(Even some that isn't there!)
Tells me stories every night -
When our fire is warm and bright.
Treats me as the child I see
When the mirror grins at me:
Muddy clothes and dirty face,
Old, scuffed shoes with broken lace.
Life could never be the same
If she weren't there to call my name . . .

Carolyn Smith

DREAMING IS FREE?

I dreamed a dream of living and doing everything I wanted to do
But then my dreams faded slowly when I met and married you
I gave you all of my life, everything that I was and wanted to be
My dreams then belonged to you, I loved you totally
My whole being ached to share all those dreams with you
But sharing didn't come naturally, you just did what you wanted to do
That sad stage of reality killed any more dreams that I may have had
My dreams all died out silently and left me feeling sad
Sad that life could do that to me when I had dreamed of so much more
Why couldn't I fulfil my dreams, what did I dream them for?

J Gatenby

LOOKING BACK

A dagger plunged deep in my heart
When wartime tore us both apart,
And the life-blood mingling with my tears
Formed a flowing river through long years.
None but my pillow shared the sorrow
As I strove to face the morrow.

Such sweet things I ponder yet . . .
The flames that kindled when we met,
Loving and loved in heavenly bliss,
The consuming passion of your kiss.

But now with age the river is dry,
And nothing is left but life's long sigh.
Times past forever linger on,
Remembering still - but the pain is gone.

And old parched lips whisper
Like soft gentle rain,
A prayer that one day
We may meet again.

Irene Locke

A Home Is . . .

A photograph taken on the day of my wedding
The bottom drawer stuff, the hated frilly bedding.
A pair of shoes she bought me for just one penny
The lies she told, 'No mummy I haven't had any.'
The bunch of flowers, fancy wrapped to ease his conscience,
Or early morning giggles when we laughed at nonsense.
The bitter fights we had when there wasn't any answer,
An affair you had when I was fighting Cancer.
The plinking sound of demijohn, you were busy making wine,
Nights of love and dreams I had you'd be forever mine.
Small corners of our home we organised together,
Expensive shoes you had to buy because they were Italian leather.
Invited friends, the food I cooked to give you pleasure,
On summer nights at yardarm time and drinking at our leisure.
Empty spaces left by you where once your clothes were hanging,
Now quiet and still as death, no movement or doors banging.
The negligee I wore to fascinate your eye,
Your busy days and night-time plays, you left me home to sigh.
But memories are made of this and housed within a home,
Walls are filled with packages you left behind to roam.
Pretending now, I fill my days, at night alone I sit,
A house becomes a home only when there is love in it.

Trish Birtill

WE - ARE THE MASTERS

What a remarkable turn-around, for us *females* - in this 20th century
No longer - do we have to swim, against the tide,
No longer - are we the underdogs, of the human species
Today - we are *dominant*, but - are we satisfied?

We can openly, walk into a *public bar* - without comment
Choose a *casual lover* - willy nilly - into our bed,
Refuse - to enter into any *permanent commitment*
And have our children, with *no* ties - like *getting wed.*

Three nights a week - off we go to *bingo*
No matter - how much the *boyfriend may object,*
And fashion-wise? We wear the shortest *mini* - all year round
Despite - having the neighbourhoods - *plumpest legs.*

With the advent of new machines - and modern gadgets
The drudgery of kitchen chores, and washday blues, have disappeared,
And should an elderly Grandma speak of the 'old days'
To today's modern *mum* - it must all sound - *a bit weird*

In the *commercial* world - many men find that
Working for a *female boss* - is the *norm*
A situation - that *not* too many moons ago
Would be ridiculed - with laughter and scorn.

When a *man* urgently needs to replace - a broken shoelace
What does he find - in his local *department store?*
A range of *ladies perfumery - lipstick* and *mascara*
The complete gamut - takes up - the *entire ground floor.*

Yes, indeed - how the role of the *modern female* has changed
From the wretched servant girl, of the 19th century, to the modern miss,
Who brazenly - will ogle any suitable bloke, in jeans
And is - certainly not adverse - to a *public kiss.*

Stella Miller

WAKE UP WITH THE HUE AND CRY OF CARS AND BUSES

City life
Wake up to the hee and cry,
Of cars and buses dashing by.
Scramble up to dress on time,
Thankful that the weather's fine.

Join the crowds all rush and tear,
Catch the bus, pay the fare.
Cross the road, takes a while,
No one seems to want to smile.

All too busy, in such haste,
Cannot stop, no time to waste.
This is dear old London Town,
When on earth will it slow down?

What will folks do with time they save?
Will they pray, or will they slave
To hurry to the pension day?
Then they spend their pence away.

On their bodies to repair,
The damage done by fast-life wear.
Slow down dear old London Street,
Life is short, but living sweet.

Vera Hilton

WOMEN - WAKE UP!

Every woman's a tragic being,
So unperfect in their eyes,
laugh, laugh, you feel alone,
grumpy mortal wake up!
Feel the sun on your face,
run like paper along the beach,
squeeze your energy and rise your chest,
and a stronger woman you shall be.
Women - wake up!

Donna Joanne Kinsey

TOUGH OLD BIRDS

We've lived too long, the young ones hint.
We've had our day; we've done our stint.
We've swallowed up the Nation's wealth
With pensions, hand-outs, National Health.

When, half-a-century ago
We went to war to stop the flow
Of evil spreading 'cross the earth,
We showed the world what we were worth.

No counselling for stress,
Or compensation for the mess
Of families torn apart by fear
Of pain and death, great danger near.

So, tough old birds we've learnt to be
Who've coped against adversity.
Don't begrudge us taking space,
Show us patience with good grace.

Corinne Lovell

The Day The World Stood Still

The day we lost Princess Diana
Was the day the world stood still.
Nobody could believe it
And nobody ever will.

Diana was loved by the young and old
She was worth her weight in gold.
She always had time for everyone
No matter what they've done.

Diana made time to visit the dying
Whether it was morning, noon or night.
She would comfort them if they were crying,
Di bought a ray of sunshine and light.

We will never again see her smiling face,
That was full of charm and full of grace.
Her golden hair and friendly stare,
Diana was someone who really did care.

Diana is now a star in the sky,
That will twinkle and shine so bright.
But until we all meet again,
For now Diana, this is *goodnight.*

Jean England

INFORMATION

We hope you have enjoyed reading this book - and that you will continue to enjoy it in the coming years.

If you like reading and writing poetry drop us a line, or give us a call, and we'll send you a free information pack.

Write to :-

WomensWords Information
1-2 Wainman Road
Woodston
Peterborough
PE2 7BU
(01733) 230746